Wisdom With
Understanding
is Better
Than Rubies

Lurine Karon Greenberg
Fine Arts Collection

paper details

Claire Richardson

photography by Polly Wreford

text contributor Elizabeth Machin

paper details

RYLAND
PETERS
& SMALL
LONDON NEW YORK

Senior designer **Sally Powell**

Senior editor **Clare Double**

Location research manager **Kate Brunt**

Location researcher **Sarah Hepworth**

Production **Gavin Bradshaw**

Art director **Gabriella Le Grazie**

Publishing director **Alison Starling**

Stylist **Claire Richardson**

First published in the United States
in 2001 by
Ryland Peters & Small, Inc.
519 Broadway
5th Floor
New York
NY 10012

www.rylandpeters.com

10 9 8 7 6 5 4 3 2 1

ISBN 1 84172 181 6

Printed and bound in China

Library of Congress Cataloging-in-Publication Data

Richardson, Claire, 1969-
  Paper details / Claire Richardson, Elizabeth Machin.
    p. cm. – (The details series)
  ISBN 1-84172-181-6
  1. Paper work. I. Machin, Elizabeth. II. Title. III. Series.

TT870 .R54 2001
745.54—dc21   2001031857

CONTENTS

introduction

Paper, part of our everyday lives and often taken for granted, is fast becoming a fashionable material for art, design, and decoration. There are papers for writing, drawing, painting, printing, wrapping, bookbinding, conservation, dressmaking, and decoration. Sheets can be textured or smooth, transparent or opaque, thick or thin, plain or patterned, white or colored, painted or printed, glossy or matt, embroidered, embossed, or embedded with flowers. Paper also appeals to the senses and is as much a feast for the fingertips as for the eyes: the rustle of crinkly candy wrappers, and the cutting, tearing, creasing, folding, curling, and flutter of paper make this the most sensuous of media to work with.

In today's hi-tech world, where e-mails are the new greeting cards, it is reassuring to know that paper remains one of the most creative means of communication—and it's available to everyone. Originally a luxury, it is now widely sold, affordable, and full of possibilities. From humble newsprint to handmade sheets, this book shows you how to discover the simple pleasure of paper—and how to make this ordinary material special. Elegant ideas and imaginative details are grouped into themes. Find fresh ideas for festive occasions, or recall childhood with paper fun for family celebrations and birthday parties. You'll see how some papers resemble fabric, and how paper lighting, screens, frames, and boxes are finding their way into the home. There is also stylish stationery, elaborate bindings for books, and winning ways with wrapping.

As far as paper is concerned, the sky is the limit!

the papers

From simple brown paper to the sheerest of handmade sheets, paper is plentiful, varied, and versatile to use. The many different kinds each have their own distinctive characteristics, and are often made for a particular purpose. You can choose from a wide range of papers to find the right one for the job at hand.

Paper has been with us for two thousand years. From its origins in China, papermaking flourished in many regions including China and Japan, India and the Himalayas, Nepal, Thailand, America, and Europe. Today the choice of machinemade and handmade paper is exhaustive, with this expressive medium enjoying a revival. Paper is so familiar that we forget that it has its source in nature, with trees providing many of the raw materials for the ever-growing paper industry. Buying recycled paper products, recycling waste paper, and supporting replanting projects all help to conserve the world's forests.

Generally speaking, paper is either handmade, moldmade, or machinemade, and its creation based on either Eastern or Western papermaking techniques and traditions. It is also made from many different fibers, including leaf and grass fibers or raw fibers like flax, while recycled fibers include old cotton and linen rags.

Handmade paper is made in individual sheets and has four ragged, or deckle, edges. Many of the finest papers are made by hand, with papermakers creating their own distinctive and even custom-made sheets.

Japan has a long tradition of making paper, known as Washi, *wa* meaning "Japan" and *shi*, "paper." Japanese paper is either handmade (Washi Tesuki) or machinemade (Washi Kikaizuki) and is made from one or varying proportions of three basic fibers known as *kozo*,

RIGHT Rolls of moldmade watercolor and printmaking paper. Not restricted to pure white, they are also available in other shades.
THIS PAGE Handmade marigold Khadi paper.

LEFT A stack of densely packed papers can be truly inspiring. You can almost feel the weight and texture of these compressed sheets of Somerset paper, a type especially made for printmaking.

gampi, and *mitsumata*. Thousands of papers are made from the robust *kozo* fibers, including Kozo Gampi Torinoko, Japan's official stationery paper. Mitsumatashi is a fine paper ideal for detail printing and etching. Some sheets are named for places and fibers, and others for their intended use—such as Kasagami, meaning "umbrella paper" and Shoji-Gami, "screen paper." Beautiful Uminami, lacelike paper with delicate spiral, snowflake, wave, and fan shapes, is breathtaking.

There is also a large range of inventive Indian papers. Handmade Khadi papers are cotton rag papers suitable for watercolor, drawing, and printmaking. These papers come in smooth and rough surfaces, and can also be primed with gesso for oil painting. Many traditional Indian papers also have natural inclusions such as tea, grass, and flower petals.

OPPOSITE A selection of papers from around the globe shows the wide variety of papers available. Soft, smooth sheets contrast with thicker, textural surfaces; the more unusual papers have natural additions like seasonal plants and flower petals. THIS PAGE Handmade pure flax paper.

Other popular papers include Nepalese Washi and Natural Mountain papers made from lokta bark plants cultivated in the hill forests of Nepal. From almost weightless to thick papers with a textured surface, these natural sheets are ideal for printmaking and collage, while the light- and medium-weight Washi is excellent for ink drawing.

Handmade papers offer a great variety of color, surface, and weight, with many full of local character. Decorative textured papers in Argentina incorporate fruit and vegetables such as slices of apple, radish, or turnip, while garlic gives a Brazilian paper a mottled look. Sensuous French papers include the soft white Fleurs,

THIS PAGE Everyday newsprint, piled high
and peppered with flecks of color, can be
imaginatively reused and transformed into
something special. Both black-and-white and colored
sheets are excellent for creative papier-mâché. This
most modest of materials is unlimited in supply and
full of unexpected possibilities.

OPPOSITE These simple sheets show
a selection of handmade Indian Khadi
papers in different textures. Khadi papers
are very strong and come in a choice
of surfaces, weights, and sizes.

containing seasonal local petals, grasses,
and leaves, while Fabriano in Italy produces
fine papers richly colored with earth
pigments from the area. In Britain, colored
and textured plant papers are often named
after their natural ingredients, such as
bracken, mulberry, and straw.

Moldmade papers resemble handmade
papers, but have only two deckle edges.
They come in a wide range of textures.
Many watercolor papers are moldmade
and are available in all shapes and
sizes, from sheets and pads to blocks
and spiral-bound books. Arches
Aquarelle and Saunders Waterford

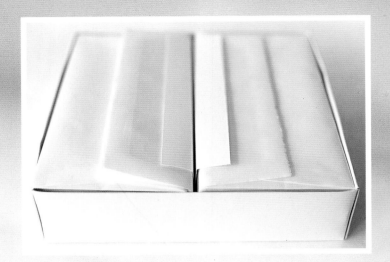

are premium watercolor papers, while for pastels, Ingres-type papers are popular, being slightly textured and tinted for subtle color harmonies.

The surfaces of handmade and moldmade paper are traditionally referred to as HP, NOT, and Rough. HP (Hot Pressed) is smooth, Rough is rough, and NOT (Not Hot Pressed) lies somewhere in between. NOT, known as Cold Pressed in the United States, is often used for watercolor painting. Handmade and moldmade papers tend to be known by their maker's watermark. A watermark is visible when the paper is held to the light. It is a sign of authenticity and can also help to identify the grade of paper.

In addition to handmade papers, there is an enormous choice of machinemade papers suitable for printing and drawing. Utility papers such as cartridge, corrugated, blotting, tracing, and tissue are now extensively made and are consistent, affordable, and widely available. There are also more experimental machinemade papers for artists and designers.

INSET ABOVE A box of fine stationery makes letter writing more personal and pleasurable.

BACKGROUND Wallpaper is not just for decorating. Rolls of your favorite machinemade or hand-printed wallpapers can cover everything from storage boxes and notebooks to more decorative frames and screens.

The home is a natural habitat for paper. In addition to making stylish stationery, paper is infinitely versatile and makes great lighting, screens, frames, and table decorations. Paper has also found its way into the closet—folded, ruffled, and stitched to make clothes, shoes, and bags.

paper
for the home

Cut frames out of thick cardboard and cover in simple, tactile papers. These white frames softly draw the eye to the black-and-white photographs while keeping the look light, airy, and uncluttered.

CREATIVE CORRESPONDENCE

stationery

Stationery has long been fashionable and, influenced by current trends, is available in all sizes and colors. From a sheaf of exquisite writing paper with handmade envelopes to vacation postcards stamped with fond memories, stationery can be chic, fun, and individual.

In this electronic age, paper is still one of the best-loved and most sensuous materials for communication: much more evocative than e-mail!

LEFT Set the scene for stationery. This antique painted desk and chair sit happily with more contemporary storage. Arrange your desk close to a window and let the natural light lift your spirits and feed your creative senses. Personalize your work space with favorite objects and freshly cut flowers.

ABOVE AND RIGHT This silver
toast rack is transformed into an
ingenious letter rack, holding
paper and envelopes. Try
contrasting textures and color
combinations, or monogrammed
items for a personal touch.

BELOW Business cards don't have to be boring. Make your own business-sized cards using monogrammed rubber stamps pressed into different-colored inks. Decorate with gold leaves cut from shiny foil for a three-dimensional effect.

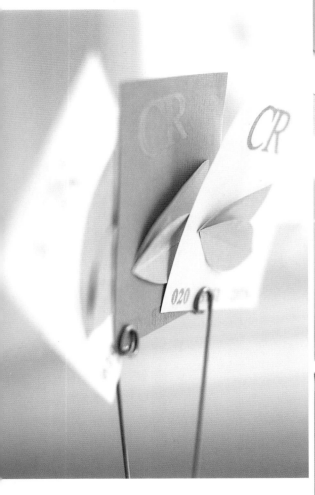

For truly elegant stationery, pick the finest papers, teamed with heavy envelopes lined in fine tissue. The addition of real gold leaf—or shiny gold foil—is the perfect finishing touch

the midas touch

The choice of custom-made and off-the-shelf stationery is enormous, ever-growing, and globally sourced. From smart modern cartridge and ecofriendly Khadi papers to fine tissue and fancy marbled sheets, stationery comes in every color, shape, texture, and size, and is often designed to mix and match—don't be restricted to plain white paper.

CENTER Design your own headed notepaper. Choose pastel sheets and decorate with gold leaf. Select easy shapes, such as small squares, stars, or flowers. Use a fine paintbrush to paint the design in acrylic gold size. Wait until the size is tacky to the touch and then apply the gold leaf.

LEFT Add a touch of fine luxury to letter writing with stylish white envelopes lined with beautifully translucent tissue in citrus, aqua, and lavender shades.

Decorative details—punched or deckle edges, pressed flowers, handmade envelopes and cards —make your message heard

decorated notepaper

Personal and business stationery for letterheads and invitations can be printed and engraved using classic or individual type styles on fine and interesting papers. Sheets can be translucent, metallic, deckle-edged, and even double-colored. Many shops also have their own brands. Browse through paper sample books at a specialized stationer and ask for their advice on any requirements that you may have. Things to consider may include different weights of paper and board, watermarks, paper design, and details such as gilding and die stamping (embossing an image on paper to produce a raised finish).

Nel Hoeg
textiles

0201 74 534 8864

In a world of electronic mail, a handmade card or decorated notepaper is a breath of fresh air

OPPOSITE Surprising contrasting textures of paper and fabric combine to create decorative business cards. Here, lightweight luster paper, printed with name and address details, is stuck to a very thin card, which is folded and finished with a fabric swatch.

LEFT Handmade envelopes make mailing letters special. Make your own from a selection of colored and textured Thai papers using envelope patterns (available from good art-supply stores). Draw around the pattern and score the guiding lines before folding and gluing.

BACKGROUND Personalize plain and patterned papers with seasonal flowers and petals. Simply decorate the top of the paper with dried and pressed flowers. Position them using a glue stick and finish each sheet by cutting with decorative paper edgers or a simple hole punch.

RIGHT Rework the humble postcard with a variety of photocopied images. Vacation snapshots, train tickets, old receipts, and natural finds can be collaged together in your own design. To transfer printed numbers directly onto a postcard, first reverse the numbers on a photocopier. Lightly spray the photocopy with hairspray. Place face down on the postcard, cover with a spare sheet of paper and apply a warm (not hot) iron. Please take care to avoid fumes, and work only in a well-ventilated area.

Plain and recycled papers make the best backgrounds to show off leaf silhouettes

natural resources

An affordable alternative to custom-made paper is to customize your own materials for correspondence. Paper, cards, and envelopes can be hand-painted with borders, cut with paper edgers, decorated with cut newsprint, or embedded with pressed flowers.

ABOVE For naturally organic business cards, print your details on brown packaging paper and stick it to thin card. Add skeleton leaves found on crisp fall walks. RIGHT For homemade paper, take a leaf from nature and color-photocopy sage, rose, or geranium leaves on brown, textured, and recycled papers.

LEFT Simple old-fashioned scrolls with a handwritten message make romantic invitations. These scrolls are made from textured Khadi papers. Roll them, finish with a traditional wax seal, and then hand-deliver.

Whether you want to send an invitation or share good news, a framed or mounted picture gets the message across. For dramatic effect, deliver a calligraphed scroll with a flourish

wish you were here

Used throughout the ages for correspondence, paper has conveyed and revealed many secrets, from love affairs to government intrigues. Now, a handwritten letter folded inside a tissue-lined envelope is a luxury.

Fresh, new paper has inspired writers and poets for generations, so make writing an enjoyable experience. Provide yourself with stacks of beautiful papers and accessories. Don't limit yourself to the papers themselves: glass and antique paperweights, colored and perfumed inks, and wonderful goose quills and reed pens are all designed to make writing feel more creative.

RIGHT Old family photographs are a great source of inspiration for making your own postcards and greeting cards. Photocopy favorite snapshots, cut out, and frame using photo corners.
OPPOSITE White paper doilies make pretty alternative borders for framing photographs.

A blank sheet is just a starting point. Gather your thoughts and let your imagination do the rest

BEAUTIFUL BINDING
books

Gather cherished memories in a journal, make the snappiest photo album, or cover notebooks with wallpaper. For personal journals, mix smooth pages with a jacket in rough Khadi paper and bind with stitching, or hole-punch and tie with string or ribbon. Decorate a garden book with leaves, flowers, and seeds, or a child's scrapbook with finds from a nature trail.

Bookbinding began in Egypt back in the fourth or fifth century, when two boards with paper in between were simply sewn together with fibrous thread. From this original Coptic binding, many more styles have evolved, and now book art is taken seriously as an art form in its own right. Today, handmade books are modern treasures—both beautiful to view and a joy to use.

OPPOSITE BELOW Photograph albums can be expensive to buy but are easy to make using simple brown paper. These were made by cutting notebook-size sheets and compiling them into small books of about twelve pages. Machine-stitch up the left-hand side and show off your favorite snapshot on the front. The larger journal has been hand-bound using natural string with a corrugated cardboard cover.

LEFT, FAR LEFT, AND BELOW There is a good selection of albums and notebooks available, made from naturally textured papers. These artists' sketchbooks are hand-bound in six sections, using moldmade, acid-free rag paper, and stitched to the spine with waxed linen thread.

RIGHT AND
OPPOSITE ABOVE
Try covering existing
notebooks with your
favorite wallpapers.
Wallpaper swatches
are cheap and often
free. Cut a sheet to
match the size of
your book, allowing
for turning margins.
Simply fold and
stick using double-
sided tape.

Use patterned or textured papers to reflect your mood or the contents of your book: addresses, baby's first year, visitors' comments, favorite recipes, or secret thoughts

creative covers

BELOW RIGHT Create a daybook using cartridge paper, hand-torn to size, with colored Khadi papers for the front and back covers. Punch two holes, about 1in (3cm) from the left-hand edge and 3in (8cm) from the top and bottom. Thread a rubber band across the back, securing to a twig in front for a rustic finish.

RIGHT Look out for special books designed with travel in mind. This Darrell Gibbs travel journal, made from assorted papers, also features translucent paper sleeves for storing travel souvenirs and mementos. Don't forget to include drawings, maps, photographs, and tickets to document your latest journey.

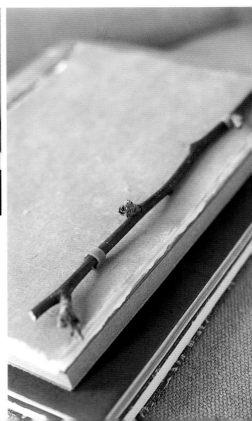

The amazing choice of books and journals now available is designed to make every occasion special. Choose from sketchpads, travel journals, diaries, daybooks, and more to celebrate birthdays, weddings, and anniversaries.

Inspirational books are accessible and affordable in the chain stores. Ordinary notebooks can easily be transformed into something special with a cover of beautiful wrapping

paper, or you can make your own
using thick brown-paper sleeves with
contrasting fine white lined sheets,
simply sewn together with thread.

For something special, many
stationers now have a custom-made
bookbinding service, offering a vast
choice of handmade papers, jackets,
and endpapers. They can also rebind
old favorites. Endpapers include the
traditional marbled papers popular in
Victorian times, while books can be
sewn together in all manner of styles.
The best materials to use will depend
on what a book is to be used for.
Whatever you choose, make sure that
everything coordinates harmoniously
and makes a pleasing whole.

Old envelopes, copies, and paper bags make truly recycled
notepads, with odd colors and textures as a bonus

a new lease on life

PRSRT STD
U.S. POSTAGE
PAID
HEBRON, OH
Permit No. 289

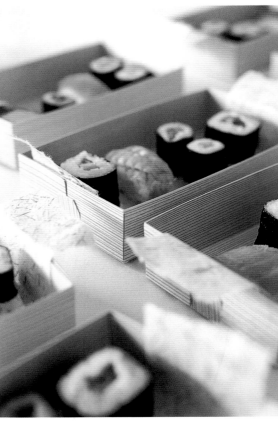

LEFT Individual boxes of chocolates in crinkly paper cases are a novel way to present after-dinner favors, and make ideal gifts for friends and family.

BELOW Make entertaining easy. An original party idea is to buy disposable paper sushi boxes. Tear strips of Thai paper to make decorative individual runners, arrange the sushi on top of the runners, and serve.

SPICK AND SPAN
boxes

Functional or fancy, boxes are an invaluable part of modern life. There are all kinds of boxes, designed for food, filing, favors, shopping, shoes, and much more. From tiny sushi trays to tall magazine files, boxes are a great and decorative way to organize your life.

We live in a time when most of us accrue more and more possessions each year. Avoid clutter by making sure everything is beautifully organized and neatly stored away. From useful shoeboxes to decorative gift boxes, this simple paper creation has become both a necessity and an indulgence.

Boxes are now big business, come in hundreds of different shapes, sizes, and colors, and are designed to store and conceal almost anything. Every item you buy nowadays seems to come in a throwaway box, from prepackaged food to electrical goods. Old cardboard boxes can be recycled and customized, ready-made gift boxes personalized for presents, storage boxes decorated with wallpaper, and favor boxes filled with edible treats.

RIGHT Homemade cookies, arranged in a simple, plain brown-paper box lined with delicate white paper doilies, make a great traditional gift. Cut single doilies in half and place in between the layers of cookies.

For home offices, keep your affairs in order with cardboard drawer dividers, diskette boxes, filing and archive boxes, suspension and box files, and pencil and pen holders covered in natural papers. Keep the look utilitarian with plenty of second-generation recycled brown cardboard and tough corrugated papers. Save space and buy boxes and shelving that are consistently sized, thus making stacking easier.

BELOW Smarten up ordinary magazine files by covering with decorative and interesting papers. Here, black-and-white photocopies of handwritten letters and old documents, found at a local flea market, were used.

TOP Many boxes, like this CD store, are made for a specific use. Covered with linen-look paper, it has a chrome handle and label card.

LEFT, BELOW, AND OPPOSITE BOTTOM RIGHT Think twice about throwing away old boxes. Cover them in different-colored papers and use to store notions, seaside finds, or whatever you like. Cut out two rectangular pieces of paper for both box and lid, allowing extra for margins. Fold the paper around the box and stick, using double-sided tape. Instead of written labels, decorate a box with shells, buttons, ribbons, or feathers, to give a clue to its contents.

A present inside a decorated box is two gifts in one. Start with a plain box and customize it to suit its contents or the recipient. Try glittery ribbon, paper flowers, or colorful sequins

glorious gift boxes

Cardboard boxes are great for anyone who is a collector or a hoarder. They can easily be painted, covered, and decorated with a glimpse of whatever is inside. Natural finds can find a home in a box painted and stenciled with a design of trailing leaves; notions boxes can be trimmed with ribbon, jewelry boxes divided into sections and fastened with a "gem," while paints and crayons can be stored in a box stamped with children's handprints.

ABOVE Choose interesting gift boxes and simply add your own finishing touches. Here a box already covered in plain matt gold paper is decorated with small colorful sequins and topped with wired beads.

RIGHT AND BELOW For party guests, try hanging tiny gift boxes tied with thread from a gilded favor tree. Fill them with sugared almonds or rose-flavored Turkish delight, and secure the contents with delicate gold ribbon.

LEFT There is a great choice of gift boxes specially made with giving in mind. Here a plain gold box has been customized using a decorative waxed paper flowerhead and bead ribbon.

Boxes make brilliant solutions to just about any storage problem. From good-sized shoeboxes and grocery cartons to pillboxes and matchboxes, you're sure to find something to fit the bill. Long-lasting and easy to stack, specially made or leftover packaging, make them as plain or pretty as you like

the classic container

BELOW Organize documents and papers into safe and sturdy archive boxes—great for the home office. Personalize with handwritten labels in contrasting papers, stuck to the front of the boxes with double-sided tape.

LEFT AND BELOW
Functional brown
boxes come in many
shapes and sizes,
but don't have to be
plain. Combine
function with a touch
of glamour: brighten
simple shoeboxes by
sticking on a colorful
Polaroid image of the
pair waiting inside.

interiors

Decorate your home with stylish handmade papier-mâché bowls, simple paper screens, and vases wrapped in Chinese papers. Forget fabric and make pretty floral paper shades, embroidered cushions, even unusual curtains and tiebacks. Use paper for perfect finishing touches.

RIGHT Not only do these delicate rose-scented incense sticks smell good, but their delicate Chinese paper packaging makes an attractive display.

RIGHT Judy
Simmons' exquisite
papier-mâché bowls
combine colored
tissue and Chinese
decorative papers.
Judy uses a plastic
or metal bowl as a
mold and builds up
layers of patterned
papers and plain
newsprint, using
watered-down
white glue as an
adhesive. When
it is completely dry,
Judy removes
the bowl from the
mold, trims the
rough edges, and
adds a simple
paper edging.

Add a bright touch to a neutral interior
with a colorful papier-mâché bowl

LEFT Papier-mâché is wonderfully versatile, as different papers offer varying textures and colors. These thin yet strong bowls by Magie Hollingworth are molded over used lamp bulbs and made from pink newspaper, giving this beautiful warm stone color.

BELOW AND RIGHT Recycled cardboard is plentiful and cheap, making it an ideal medium for furniture designers. This simple modern screen is both a practical and decorative way of dividing space. It is also used here to hang framed black-and-white photos.

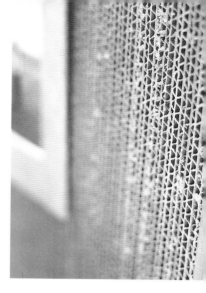

Yesterday's news becomes today's papier-mâché bowls, while recycled cardboard boxes become practical room dividers

a new life for old paper

Traditionally, the only paper you would find in the average home was on the walls. Now, wallpaper is once again becoming chic, and paper itself is the latest material to be found in the fashion-conscious home. Designers are experimenting with paper to make inventive lighting, screens, frames, rugs, storage, bowls, shelving, furniture, and even soft furnishings.

Paper screens have long been a familiar sight in Japanese homes.
Try making your own semitransparent paper shade to block out
an ugly view, or create a delicate screen or airy room divider
using colorful Indian tissue-paper garlands

dividing space

There is a growing range of papers which, surprisingly, are strong enough to be used in interior decoration. Paper screens are a familiar sight in Japanese homes and are now finding their way into other contemporary settings. Both beautiful and practical, screens are a versatile way of dividing space and providing a decorative feature. Styles vary tremendously, from recycled cardboard and papier-mâché to sheer Japanese paper.

LEFT Many papers resemble fabrics and can make effective shades. Here, semitransparent Japanese paper has been decorated with flowers cut from poppy-red Khadi paper. Cut the sheet to fit your window frame and reinforce the top and bottom of the shade with a strip of thicker cartridge paper. Use double-sided tape to stick the edges to the window frame.

THIS PAGE Dress up living spaces with this easy-to-make paper-flower curtain. Unravel individual garlands of tissue-paper flowers, made for Indian weddings. Attach the ends to a garden stake (space the garlands about 4in (10cm) apart). Then hang the stake inside a doorframe.

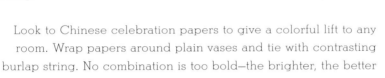

Look to Chinese celebration papers to give a colorful lift to any
room. Wrap papers around plain vases and tie with contrasting
burlap string. No combination is too bold—the brighter, the better

instant color tonic

Papier-mâché is both a stylish and ecofriendly way of
using paper within the home. Ordinary old newsprint
and recycled paper can be transformed by this simple
technique into works of art such as bowls, decorative
vases, and frames. (See Judy Simmons' bowl on page
47.) Different types of paper produce contrasting effects
and color ranges, some more subtle than others. A
variety of everyday objects can be used as molds for
papier-mâché, from light bulbs to plastic mixing bowls
lined with plastic wrap. When dry, papier-mâché can be
painted, covered with gesso, then gilded and varnished,
making it extremely durable.

Some pliable and tactile paper fabrics are strong enough to
make soft furnishings. Cushion and bolster covers, shades,
simple curtains, and tiebacks are all possibilities

romantic flowers and fabrics

OPPOSITE Liven up plain white paper curtains with blowsy paper peonies. Libby Lister makes paper flowers with hand-tinted crêpe papers. She cuts out individual petals and molds them to shape over the back of a spoon. They are wired together using brass jewelers' wire, and finished with painted sisal string for stamens.

LEFT AND BELOW These beautifully simple pillow covers were made out of embroidered paper and lined with a colored linen.

Following the current fashion for texture and surface interest, there is now a growing selection of soft and tactile paper fabrics available. They are strong enough to be used in interiors and can even be sewn to make soft furnishings. Curtains, tiebacks, shades, bolsters, and cushions can all be made from paper fabric. The paper fabrics on the market range from plain white to crinkled, colored, and embroidered.

LEFT There is a huge variety of Japanese-style hanging paper light shades. Perfect for a bedroom, the paper on this simple cylindrical one has been molded around a soft wire framework to give a subtle pleated shape.

OPPOSITE Mini lights don't have to be left plain but can be given simple paper shades. These contemporary paper cubes are made of handmade Lokta-bark paper. Lined up on the mantelpiece, they make a warm and relaxing focal point.

BELOW A chic contemporary light. Small triangles were cut in the paper shade in a regular pattern (use a craft knife) and then pushed open to add sparkle and originality.

Illuminate your home in unusual and original ways with paper lighting. Explore the possibilities of paper accessories for specific functions, decoration, accent spotlights, or ambience. There are many ways to bring light into your life, but first of all think what your room will be used for and what kind of mood you wish to create.

Paper diffuses light, while light plays with paper's patterns and textures, making it a perfect medium for illuminating your home. From Indian paper lanterns to magical mini lights and sculptural floor lamps, paper lighting is never merely functional.

BRIGHT IDEAS

lighting

RIGHT Add color and zest to children's rooms with cheap-and-cheerful paper lighting. For a modern take on a traditional shape, this printed cardboard star has a cutout design lined with fine tissue paper, creating a colorful glow.

Lighting plays an important part in any decorative scheme. For work, use lights that are both functional and lovely to look at; while in living spaces, combine floor and ceiling lights with sculptural paper lamps to create a mixture of lighting that looks just as good at night as during the day. Hanging a line of translucent paper pendants over your dining table not only gives a softer glow, but adds interest and sparks conversation. Be inventive and adventurous with your lighting. Mini tree lights are not just for Christmas—they can be customized with paper shades for instant glamour or hung behind a sheer screen to give a dreamy starlit effect.

Children love bright colors and funky shapes, so try a beehive or star-shaped lamp, or a string of miniature paper drums along a shelf, to cast a reassuring glow in a child's room

magical moods for bedtime

ABOVE Create a magical atmosphere and breathe new life into kids' shelving with Shiu-Kay Kan's collapsible paper drums, colored vivid fuchsia, pink, and lilac.

RIGHT A small table lamp with a beehive shade has been customized in a fun and cost-effective way. Cut brightly colored tissue-paper spots and glue them to the plain white shade in a random pattern.

Colorful flower lights or a standing lamp in a bold paper shade can make a decorative focus for any room in the home. They diffuse a warm, intimate light that will complement any interior

a warm glow inside

Paper lanterns are now popular and plentiful, and can be brightly colored and magical, or white and Zen-inspired. Many Eastern-style shades are based on the shapes of traditional Japanese lanterns, painted red with bold black calligraphy. Paper pendant shades can also create a gentle, diffused light that is ideal for bedrooms.

Take paper lanterns outside and make summer parties magical after dark, or transform glass votive holders by wrapping them in a colored paper sleeve. Simple paper bags glow when filled with sand and lit by votive candles in a glass jar.

LEFT Great for a modern space, this original floor lamp makes a bold design statement. Made from a combination of Thai handmade papers and stretched over a metal frame, this sculptural lamp gives color, shape, and definition to the room.

THIS PAGE These wonderfully
sophisticated paper-flower
lights, handmade using crêpe
paper, are another variation on
the classic mini tree light. These
exotic flowers are lighting a
fireplace, but will add glamour
to any interior.

OPPOSITE Make light work of summer dining by using disposable paper table accessories and decorations in mouthwatering orchid pinks and powder blues. Throwaway white paper cloths can be transformed with simple runners made from fine Thai tissue papers.

ALL SET FOR DINNER
tables

You don't need expensive china and antique linen to set imaginative tables. Instead, choose paper designs and decorations to set the scene for warm weekend celebrations.

Make dining a talking point by introducing different cultures and traditions to your table. Decorate simple wooden chairs with tissue-paper flowers or contrast translucent porcelain bowls with woven paper placemats. Cover tables with Thai or Japanese papers, and line with intimate paper candle bowls to light up the night. They look magical during the day and give a gentle glow to long, lazy summer evenings.

Summer dining should be a casual affair with throwaway white paper cloths dressed in colored Japanese paper runners. Most of us think of white as the natural color for table settings, but brighten it with seasonal colors.

RIGHT Don't limit decorations to the table. Extend the focus of attention by hanging pleated-paper lanterns in brilliant shades of rose and fuchsia to lift the eye above the table. BELOW Mix different shades of brightly colored napkins, pile them high, and weigh down with a seaside pebble. Continue the decorative theme by decorating the stone with a square of Chinese silver paper.

RIGHT Spruce up simple wooden chairs by decorating with tissue-paper flowers. These combine six layers of tissue paper in three shades of pink, with wired sequins holding the center of the flower. Begin with a starter kit. OPPOSITE Pierre Pozzi's amazing paper trays are formed out of standard brown paper and make the perfect vehicle for carrying trays of drinks. Decorate wineglasses with wired crêpe-paper leaves.

Extras—a mix of napkins, a handmade paper
flower, or decorated glass—make dining a treat

color-coordinated details

LEFT Pure white woven paper placemats make a great textural contrast to sleek porcelain bowls. Continue the table's theme by adding appliquéd flowers in intense fuchsia pink. Cut petals from patterned tissue paper, stick with diluted white glue, and when dry secure by stitching on a sewing machine. BELOW To complete the theme, give guests individually wrapped chopsticks. Cut rectangles of paper about 6in (15cm) x 3in (8cm). Fold around a pair of chopsticks and glue at the top and along the side, folding and tucking in the opening front edge. Decorate using a square of Chinese silver paper. OPPOSITE Transform everyday plastic garden pots quickly and easily by wrapping with forget-me-not blue lokta paper, tied with natural raffia. Plant simple greenery like this *Selaginella* in the pots and arrange along the length of the table.

Try mixing country-style furniture with traditional Japanese trimmings

east meets west

Add contrast with pots of glossy green foliage, wrapped in paper and tied with string.

Give gatherings for family and friends a personal touch with handwritten name cards, or make pretty place settings by gluing summer petals to folded watercolor paper. Think of fresh ways to present after-dinner mints, and try giving paper bundles filled with fortune cookies, homemade chocolates, or sugared almonds as favors for guests.

You could continue the Eastern theme by serving drinks in unusual glasses entwined with paper leaves, arranged on trays decorated with sheets of handmade Japanese papers.

Neat boxes with individual treats inside, or a pile
of wrapped candy in a bowl, are sure to please

fortunes and favors

OPPOSITE Present after-dinner
mints in small paper bundles
piled in an elegant porcelain
bowl. Cut individual pieces of
Japanese Hikakushi paper
around 6in (15cm) square, fill
with mint chocolates or bonbons,
pull all four corners together,
and tie with linen string.

LEFT AND BELOW These simple
pail-shaped boxes with wire
handles are a great idea for
presenting fortune cookies and
for holding guests' name cards.
Fortune cookies not only
reinforce the Eastern theme,
they also provide a great
talking point for guests.

ABOVE AND RIGHT These
mules were inspired by an
original paper-shoe pattern.
Made with cardboard soles and
medium-weight Thai decorative
paper uppers, they were
customized with rhinestone
studs and a pink paper lining.

OPPOSITE TOP Andrea
Joynson's delicate paper
handbag makes ingenious use
of crinkled paper fabric. This
softly tactile bag has been
hand-embroidered with
individual flowerheads and
machine-stitched together.

Paper fashion is no fantasy. Leaf through the pages of costume history, and you'll find Fortuny dresses made from pleated Japanese paper. The Japanese have long used paper on the pockets of kimonos or for pleated and painted fans. Elsewhere, paper costumes and masks brighten carnivals and festivals. Today, fashion designers are discovering paper as a new material.

Paper, like fabric, can be sewn and sequinned, and is a great medium for displaying designers' inventiveness. You can buy paper fabric to add to those papers that are adaptable for fashion, such as wispy tissue paper for lace or paper doilies for cuffs and collars. Paper can be trimmed with braids, beads, and ruffles, or whatever you fancy.

Ordinary papers can inspire fashion design—and details make all the difference. Like fabric, paper can be stitched, folded, and embroidered, making it a fashionable material for designers. Hats, handbags, shoes, and even dresses are now made out of specialized papers, so take this simplest of materials and give it a twist.

TACTILE TEXTILES

fashion

Why not reinterpret the latest styles,
or recreate fashion history with paper?

all the trimmings

Painting can give plain paper the look of textured fabric, as well
as creating the illusion of movement. Loose strokes on paper give
the impression of fabric falling in folds, or drag paint across paper
with a wavy comb for "taffeta." For period costumes, paint or stencil
detailed flowers on decorative papers to resemble hand embroidery.
Milliners mold paper for hats and decorate with paper ribbons,
bows, and flowers. Alternatively, trim your own hat with paper details.

THIS PAGE Lynn Dennison's amazing
decorative paper shoes are handmade
from white Japanese tissue paper on a
fine sculptural wire structure, dressed
with elaborate red gems.

OPPOSITE LEFT Modeled on a 1920s slip
pattern, this crinkly paper dress has an air
of faded glamour. The fabric's lacy floral
design is echoed in the antique doily used
at neck and hem.

OPPOSITE RIGHT The flower detail on the
neckline of the dress was made from a floral
doily. Cut out six individual flowers, stack,
and pin at the center with wire and beads.

Paper is an endlessly versatile material for millinery—
although not recommended for rainy days—and bags, too

handy hats and handbags

There are now even patterns for paper shoes; try making your own simple mules,
or commission some custom-made stilettos—for decoration only! These days,
handbags come in new shapes for each season, and take on a whole new feeling
when made from interesting papers. Straw baskets are rewoven with textured,
recycled papers. Visit costume galleries, and hat and bag stores, for inspiration.

LEFT AND TOP This tactile basket is woven
from layers of newsprint. Modern handles
add a practical and simple contrast, making
the basket useful for shopping and storage.
ABOVE AND RIGHT Adorn a basic paper hat
with a broad crêpe-paper ribbon, leaves, and
flowers. For parties, add beads and sequins.

Give presents a personal touch with individual, imaginative wrappings. Even a humble offering is transformed into a thoughtful gift when beautifully wrapped. Accompany presents with unusual gift tags, or personalize them with handmade labels. Cards are easy to make and can be decorated with pressed leaves, seasonal foliage, or, for Christmas, frosty festive shapes.

paper
for giving

White on white always looks stylish and fresh. Delicate and sculptural paper ribbons are easy to cut from white bond paper. Here they are decorated with a fine-gauge hole punch.

78 **paper** for giving

PASS THE PRESENT

wrapping

Giftwrapping has become an art, and the wrapping paper as beautiful as the gift inside. From simple bunches of different-colored tissue to the sheer extravagance of handmade sheets, wrapping adds interest and a touch of glamour to any present.

The wonderful choice of wrappings available means choosing the right paper is just as exciting as finding the right present. Browsing in stores filled with papers is always enjoyable. But the fun doesn't stop there—how to wrap the gift is almost an art in itself.

OPPOSITE Opening gifts should be fun for both children and adults. Layer different sheets of colored tissue paper, reminiscent of pass-the-present days.
TOP LEFT Attention to detail is the key ingredient when wrapping for friends, so let your imagination run wild. Bright contrasting papers work well together and provide a brilliant backdrop for multicolored ribbons, sequins, and gilded cake ribbons.
LEFT Layer different papers and textures for contrasting effects. Add sequins to give an eclectic, opulent look.

If your gift is a prickly leaved plant or a perishable cake, don't try to hide it—let its shape inspire you. Use tissue wrap with zigzag edges for a spiky plant, or a bright handmade border for a classic white cake

a star presentation

In Japan the pleasure of receiving a present is heightened by the charm of the wrapping, with a folded message or tiny greeting included in the package. This delightful custom can transform the ordinary into a precious gift.

Imaginative papers, gift boxes, and decorative details can also reflect the personality of the giver or recipient. Take this idea farther and customize wrappings with handwriting, painting, stamping, or stenciling. Add trimmings around boxes, brighten with braid, or finish with a crinkly paper flower.

OPPOSITE LEFT Unusual shapes are often the most cumbersome to wrap. Don't be too preoccupied with disguising the gift if this proves too difficult. Giftwrapping is for presenting a gift as well as just hiding it. Plants look wonderful wrapped in swathes of contrasting tissue and wrapping paper. Decorate with broad paper ribbons, braids, and delicate Indian mirrors.

OPPOSITE RIGHT Paper edgers and pinking shears make giving an elaborate, decorative edge to your wrapping easy. If you don't have these, take the plunge and cut edges free-style.

ABOVE AND LEFT Reminiscent of a Native American's headdress, this cake has been decorated to give as a gift. A broad band of blue tissue paper has been edged with gold leaves and lace, with a contrasting green tissue ribbon placed down the center.

LEFT Take inspiration from the world around you and give your wrappings a natural theme. There are hundreds of beautiful papers that incorporate leaves, grasses, berries, flowers, and fibers from many different plants. Mix them with simple brown packaging paper and textured sheets, securing packages with natural raffia and burlap twine.

Keep paper simple, and pile on natural accessories—shells look good hanging from burlap or linen string

simply natural neutrals

OPPOSITE Concentrate on layering a variety of tones and textures when wrapping gifts. This plain russet band works well against the cream and rust paper, providing both definition and continuity. A double bow of colored raffia adds the finishing touch.

OPPOSITE INSET Versatile brown paper can make a decorative ribbon. Cut narrow strips around 1in (3cm) wide and fold into pleats. Decorate using various-gauge hole punches and cut the edges with pinking shears. To fasten it to your gift, thread with raffia or fine ribbon, and tie.

RIGHT Named after its secret ingredient, the mango leaf, this indigo paper is impressive, with a ribbon made from cream textured wave paper. The deep blue is repeated in a fastening of navy linen string, decorated with a selection of hanging shells.

LEFT Go completely green and recycle old newspapers and magazines for wrappings. Not only are you doing your bit for saving the planet, but they'll also look unique.

OPPOSITE Photocopies, either black-and-white or color, create many giftwrapping possibilities. Enlarge favorite photographs of plants and flowers, beach houses, sunsets, people, or pets.

BELOW Use rubber stamps to provide a quick and cheap alternative to designer wrapping paper. The effects can be bold or subtle, depending upon the papers and paint colors you choose. Here, an oak-leaf motif has been stamped onto brown paper, and a paisley pattern onto sky-blue mulberry paper from Thailand.

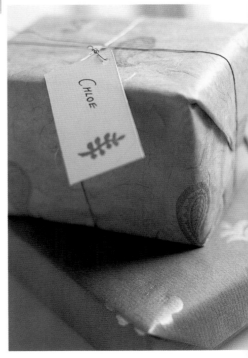

Look at newspaper, old maps, and brown paper in a new light: they could make original giftwrapping

charting new territory

Paper can also hint at the nature of the present inside. Garden gifts may be wrapped in paper pressed with dried flowers, embedded with berries, or painted with gold leaf. Jewelry could be hidden in a box fastened with a stud, or perfume may be wrapped in scented or floral paper.

ABOVE RIGHT The appeal of maps is almost magical, so why not share that magic with your friends? Out-of-date maps are ideal, but color photocopies cost about the same as sheets of wrapping paper. Finish with linen thread decorated with feathers.

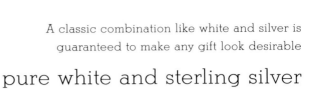

A classic combination like white and silver is guaranteed to make any gift look desirable

pure white and sterling silver

ABOVE There are some truly inspiring hand-finished papers around. This hand-distressed silver sheet has a modern hardness which contrasts well with the softness of downy feathers and matt silver balls.

RIGHT Silver and white can be an ethereal combination. Plain white paper shopping bags become instantly chic when accessorized with a diamanté buckle. Simply use a craft knife to make holes in the bag, thread with a ribbon, and decorate with a buckle. Stick the ribbon to the inside of the bag with double-sided tape.

LEFT An elegant Japanese Yuki paper ribbon. Fold a strip 3in (8cm) wide into pleats. Cut the ends to a point for the zigzag effect and decorate with a fine-gauge hole punch. Thread two pieces of silver wire through the ribbon; use to secure to the gift. BELOW Sheer paper drawstring bags are perfect for delicate or oddly shaped gifts like lingerie. Thread with luxurious ribbon and decorate with bead tassels.

Try using more than one type of paper and layering contrasting wrappings for original effects. Place fine Japanese lace papers over deep-colored crêpe, or wrap boxes in bright tissue and enclose in acetate. There are also many new takes on "brown paper packages tied up with string." Brown paper isn't boring, but a blank canvas just waiting to be painted.

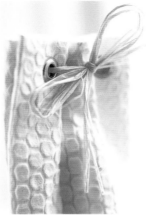

LEFT Bottle bags are a handy solution for wrapping wine and liquor, and are widely available in a huge choice of decorative papers. The simplicity of this honeycomb textured paper is repeated with a simple eyelet and raffia fastening.

RIGHT Bottles are easy to wrap using an envelope of pretty Japanese handmade paper. The circle design on this one is complemented with a decorative ribbon of gold paper punched with round holes. White feathers add a flamboyant gesture.

ABOVE Perfect for Christmas, this star-shaped box proves that gift boxes really do come in all shapes and sizes. Decorate and tie with a tangle of frothy paper ribbon, curled with a paperknife.

Simply stamp or stencil with your favorite motif using colored inks. Surprising combinations also work well, so contrast plain brown paper with bright-patterned braid, or make a lacy trim from paper cut with scallop-edged scissors, hole-punched, and threaded with ribbon.

Customize readymade containers, or make your own
flamboyantly decorated bottle bags for extra fizz

unbeatable bottles and boxes

A gift of gilded fruit
has been wrapped in a
Japanese Matsuyuki paper,
decorated with gold and
silver flecks. Choose special
threads, such as this silver
lurex thread, for tying gifts.

SIGNED, SEALED, DELIVERED

gift tags

Eye-catching gift tags are easy to make using the great choice of papers and cards now available. Labels can be customized by simply stamping the recipient's initials onto individual handmade papers, or by painting names onto plain baggage labels. Experiment with different shapes, cut decorative edges, and contrast textured papers for stylish gift tags.

RIGHT Maps and old plans are a good source of decorative material for gift tags. A simple white rectangular placecard provides a perfect frame for this section of color-photocopied map. Continue the map theme with color photocopies for sheets of giftwrap.

Gift tags play an intrinsic part in the art of wrapping, adding both a practical and personal finishing touch to a present. You can buy gift tags that are designed to coordinate with your wrapping, or create your own using unusual papers and original techniques.

90 **paper** for giving

Plain baggage tags can be transformed in an instant by cutting out shapes using a craft knife and transferring a reversed photocopy of your friend's name. Lightly spray the front of the photocopy with hairspray and place face down on the luggage label. Cover with another piece of paper and apply a warm (not hot) iron. Please do this in a well-ventilated area.

OPPOSITE RIGHT
Photocopies of favorite carols and sheets of music make great labels for Christmas gifts. Glue the copied sheet to medium-weight card and cut out a star or shape of your choice.

Gift tags in simple shapes—stars, leaves, or flowers—go well with contrasting bold colors. With the brightest wrapping and ribbons, these gifts won't go astray

bright and bold

Be imaginative when thinking about labels and how they can reflect the nature of the gift you are giving. Trace a leaf on colored paper to make greetings for gifts of plants, photocopy your favorite hymn sheets for holiday presents, or use perfumed papers embroidered with the names of the bride and groom for weddings. Even scraps of ordinary brown paper can be turned into luxurious labels by decorating with gold leaf and tying with silk ribbon.

LEFT AND ABOVE Self-adhesive labels look enchanting with hand-painted borders. Use artists' watercolor or gouache paints and a fine brush to paint flowers, stripes, spots, and waves.

ABOVE RIGHT Labels don't have to be a conventional shape. Perfect for presenting plants, these Thai paper flowers are cut using pinking shears and stuck with tape onto a thick wire. The finishing touch is a glass gem stuck within each petal.

OPPOSITE BOTTOM Combining different textures of paper can look beautiful. Here, fine tracing paper, patterned Indian wrapping paper, and a matt gold paper star are held together with a sheer pink ribbon.

OPPOSITE TOP LEFT Mix clashing colors. The fluorescent pink of this gift label looks stunning next to the vibrant orange and lime ribbon on the package. For holiday spirit, add gold paper stars.

OPPOSITE TOP CENTER Keep designs simple when designing gift tags and cards. This basic leaf shape works well with contrasting colors of lightweight card.

OPPOSITE TOP RIGHT Plain folded gift cards are easy to jazz up by cutting out a shape using a craft knife. Cut a square of contrasting tissue paper and glue it to the inside of the card.

BELOW LEFT Simple ideas are often the most charming. Rubber-stamping is a time-saving way of decorating gift tags and labels. This beanstalk motif printed on a cream card with gold ink looks chic, feminine, and romantic.

BELOW RIGHT Too good to throw away, these extravagant gold gift cards are decorated with cutout designs and lined with translucent baking parchment.

RIGHT Papyrus is wonderfully crisp and translucent. Adorned with a gilded oak leaf and raffia bow, this papyrus paper tag adds sophistication to a plain gift.

OPPOSITE Once again, draw inspiration from old letters and scripts. Use them to cover placecards to use as gift labels. Punch a hole in one corner, thread with raffia, and add a strip of papyrus paper for writing your friend's name.

Delicate cutout motifs and translucent papyrus paper and baking parchment are the perfect ingredients for sophisticated, elegant gift tags

clearly labeled

There are many plain cards on the market for you to customize. These recycled cards with cutout centers have been adorned with a square of white cotton relief paper and enhanced with a sprig of rowan leaves.

OPPOSITE Making your own cards should be fun. It also helps if you are a hoarder. These plain white cards are decorated with a rectangle of natural paper and simple beach finds. Stick pebbles to the card using a hot-glue gun, taking care not to touch the glue. Make sure objects are not so heavy that the card won't stand up.

LEFT Papyrus paper, made from the stem pith of the papyrus plant, was used by the ancient Greeks, Egyptians, and Romans. Its tactile appeal is obvious. It looks amazing decorated with complementary finds—pressed leaves, flowers, and feathers.

GROOVY GREETINGS
cards

Choose from the stylish selection of cards now available, or simply make your own. Chinese and Japanese papers, roughly torn and stuck onto handmade card, make colorful greetings, or follow the natural route using textured papers, folded or stitched together and decorated with pressed leaves, flowers, or feathers.

RIGHT Rubber-stamping is the perfect quick solution for handmaking a large quantity of festive cards. Print stars, crowns, holly, and doves in gold paint on cream paper. Cut out these stamped images into individual squares or rectangles and glue them to readymade metallic greeting cards.

OPPOSITE Three-dimensional cards are easy to make. Start with a plain greeting card like these gold and silver ones. Open it, and pencil an outline of half a Christmas tree on the inside left-hand page next to the fold. Use a cutting mat and craft knife to score along the design. Open the tree out for the completed effect.

BELOW Lorraine Dawkins makes beautiful celebration cards using Chinese papers from her local Chinese supermarket. She tears the papers into squares, using a metal ruler as a guide, and collages them onto a handmade card, securing with raffia stitches.

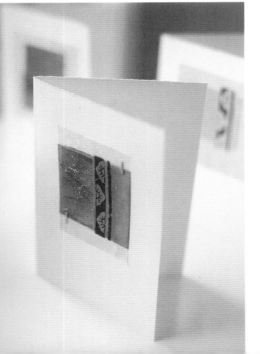

Start with a plain card and choose from rubber-stamping, collage, découpage, or three-dimensional scoring to make your greeting card stand out from the crowd

make your mark

Cards are no longer reserved to celebrate birthdays and Christmas. There are cards for Easter, engagements and weddings, a new home or a new baby, moving job and retiring, saying thank you, good luck, sorry, and much more. A pleasing image and conventional words may not satisfy your creative urges. Today, cards are designed for every occasion and styled to meet all our individual tastes.

Transform a plain card
with a cutout three-
dimensional design

RIGHT Photocopied images can be transferred onto cards using a transfer medium. Simply take a good-quality photocopy of the image you want to transfer, cut it to size, and place it on a piece of waxed paper or tinfoil. Squeeze a thick layer of transfer medium onto the picture and spread evenly, thickly enough to obscure the image. Place the print paste side down on your card or postcard. Press lightly. Let it dry for at least four hours. Place a damp (not dripping) sponge on the image and gently rub away the top layer of photocopy paper, taking care not to rub too hard and damage the card. When your image is apparent, leave the card to dry again.

Transfer a photocopied image or expose natural images onto cards using light-sensitive paper. Go beyond conventional photography to discover a new world of light and shade

photographic magic

While reproductions of famous paintings are still popular images for greetings, cards are now following the fashion for handcrafted designs using unusual papers and all sorts of decorations. Contemporary artists and textile designers often market their own special series of distinctive

ABOVE Lorraine Dawkins' silk-screened images are taken from a variety of sources including old photographs. Printed onto thick tracing paper, they are cut to size and added to cards with colored tape.
LEFT Nature Print paper produces wonderful images, perfect for card making, using only natural sunlight. Simply place leaves on the light-sensitive paper for up to two minutes and leave to expose naturally. Rinse the paper under water for a few seconds, and as if by magic, the image will appear.

handmade cards, using a mixture of printing techniques, drawing, and collage to produce a unique design.

Making and decorating cards is a rewarding pastime. Explore the different papers available, contrasting tones and textures to make your greetings special. Create surprising and sensitive combinations, mixing translucent papers with an airy feel, such as tissue and tracing papers, with strong textural board. When cutting, take care using a craft knife. Always use a cutting mat.

Cutout letters and motifs or inset designs enliven plain cards, while the card itself doesn't have to be restricted to a simple rectangle or square

glittery stars and crowns

ABOVE Initials and monograms are an attractive theme. These lilac cards have had monograms cut into them, using a craft knife and cutting mat. Silver paper has been stuck behind the cutout letters.

LEFT Branch out from standard square or rectangular cards. Crowns are easy to cut, and are a great shape to decorate with different glitters and paints.

OPPOSITE Suspend stars within greeting cards for a magical effect. Cut two stars from lightweight silver cardboard and stick together, with a thread of monofilament between their centers. Use tape to stick this thread to the inside of the card, at the top and bottom of the card's window.

Theme celebration cards. A personal
passion for handbags or shoes can
provide material for a whole range of ideas.
Photocopy favorite images and use them
in a collage on hand-trimmed cards.

LEFT Khadi rag paper makes the most tactile of postcards. Continue the textural theme by decorating with photocopied natural images such as pebbles, sand, sky, trees, and leaves.

BELOW Photographs transferred onto acetate also make great postcards and cards. Easily accessible from your local color-copy shop, acetate copies look equally good with light filtering through them or mounted on a plain white card.

adding the best backing

Every picture tells a story, but the background is just as important. Hand-trimmed cards, rag paper, and clear acetate are good choices

Blank cards can also be customized with notions, seasonal flowers, and familiar photographs, which can reflect the personality of the receiver or be themed to suit the occasion. Birth announcement cards might use a handprint or footprint stamp, while for nuptials papers infused with scented petals make a welcome change to wedding bells.

Always a popular favorite, here traditional paper chains have been updated using white paper links, some decorated with cutout diamond shapes. Suspend soft metallic paper lanterns from the chain for a modern twist on the East meets West theme.

paper for special occasions

Paper is great for inspiring fresh ideas on traditional themes. Wrap up your home for holiday with heavenly homemade stars and wreaths, decorate Easter bonnets with lacy paper-doily flowers, and make colorful cutout hearts for Valentine's Day. Rediscover the simple pleasure of paper bunting for kids' parties and witches' hats for Halloween.

STARS AND STOCKINGS

holiday

From paper chains to jeweled stars and bright wrappings, much of the remembered excitement of the season involves paper. Childhood memories come to life with cutout paper wreaths, stockings, and presents waiting to be unwrapped.

These wonderful stars are made from gold cardboard and parchment paper. Cut out three star shapes: two cardboard, one parchment paper. Carefully cut out a star within each cardboard star using a craft knife. Glue the three stars together, with the parchment paper in the center. Finally, decorate with colored glass gems.

ABOVE These brown cardboard prisms, available from good craft suppliers, make a great natural base to decorate with shiny sequins and stars. Apply white glue with a fine brush and add festive shapes.

OPPOSITE For a unique look at Christmastime, search for a more unusual tree to decorate. This old gnarled branch makes a wonderfully rustic alternative, and would look equally good sprayed either white or silver.

The giving and receiving of gifts reflects the true spirit of the holiday season. Preparing for Christmas and making paper decorations is a fun way to bring the whole family together. The day itself is a magical time for children to unwrap presents found inside homemade paper stockings.

For a truly traditional Christmas, light altar candles for a scented, warming winter glow and dress your tree with hand-decorated paper balls and delicate cutouts of

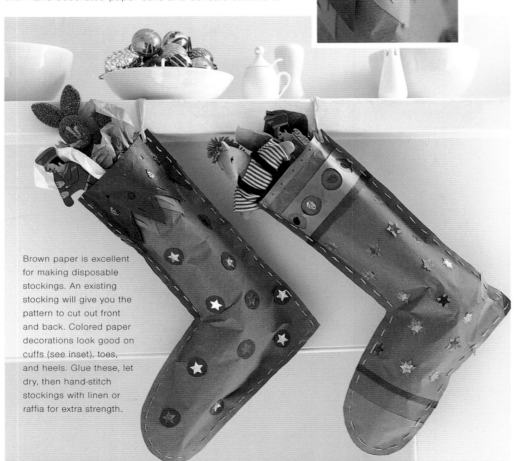

Brown paper is excellent for making disposable stockings. An existing stocking will give you the pattern to cut out front and back. Colored paper decorations look good on cuffs (see inset), toes, and heels. Glue these, let dry, then hand-stitch stockings with linen or raffia for extra strength..

stars and other festive shapes. For country-style celebrations, make paper wreaths topped with gilded berries and rosehips, or create a seasonal evergreen garland twined with paper ribbon.

Paper makes great stockings, wreaths, and decorations, as well as wrapping for gifts

not just for wrapping

ABOVE AND RIGHT Wreaths don't have to be green. This decorative wreath uses paper "oak leaves" cut from photocopies of an old document. Some were sprayed with gold artists' paint to match the rosehips. Leaves and rosehips were threaded with jewelers' wire and attached to a circular wire frame. Never leave lit candles unattended.

EXTRAORDINARY EGGS

Easter

Brightly colored cardboard, and crêpe and tissue papers, are always popular for making and decorating Easter bonnets. Paint eggs like china, or cover them in scraps of colored paper.

ABOVE Quick to make and great fun for children, these papier-mâché egg necklaces are brilliant for Easter parties and parades. You can buy the eggs from good craft shops. Paint them with cold-water dyes or inks and, when dry, decorate with colored glitter. Finally, string onto elastic using a large darning needle, and intersperse with pastel beads.

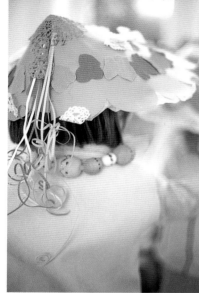

THIS PAGE Cheap and accessible art and poster papers make great Easter bonnets. For the basic shape, cut a circle of paper about 16in (40cm) in diameter. Cut a slit into the center of the circle and mold it into a hat shape around the head of a child. When happy with the size of your bonnet, secure using double-sided tape. Line with lacy paper doilies or cake holders, and decorate using contrasting papers, streamers, and ribbons.

Easter welcomes the return of springtime with children's parties, simnel cakes, colorful bonnets, and the outdoor hunt for Easter eggs. Fancy paper hats and baskets filled with speckled painted eggs resting on shredded paper are part of the mysteries of childhood. Easter bonnets can be

LEFT Paper cake holders make fabulous skirts for eggcups. Simply cut all the way around for a fringed-paper look.

THIS PAGE Replace paper shelf borders that have been around for years. To get the size and shape you like, make a template using scrap paper. Here, a scalloped design was cut from a strip of pure white cartridge paper and decorated using a multisize hole punch.

made out of all kinds of scraps of paper, from colored cardboard to paper cake cases and delicate doilies. Follow a fresh palette of golden daffodil and primrose yellows, pastel pinks, and leafy greens, to celebrate the return of spring after the long winter months.

LEFT AND BELOW Bring fresh ideas to the arts of egg decoration and découpage using scraps of wrapping and origami papers. First hard-boil and dye the eggs using cold-water fabric dyes or inks. Let them dry. Cut flowers, stripes, waves, and spots from the papers and glue them to the eggs. Apply white glue using a fine paintbrush.

Far too special just to hide in the backyard, hand-decorated eggs in fresh spring colors should take pride of place at any Easter table

egg hunt

PETALS AND POSIES

Valentine's
Day

Fun and fiery cutout paper cupids and hearts
painted in hot colors make great Valentine's
Day cards. Or design a red-paper photo album
to capture those precious moments.

Saint Valentine is the patron saint of lovers.
Unashamedly sentimental and truly romantic,
Valentine's Day is one day of the year when
we can express our true feelings. The
Victorians loved the idea and celebrated this
special occasion by sending embossed cards,
inscribed with flowery sentiments, and posies

LEFT AND OPPOSITE Make Valentine's morning
a real treat for your loved one with a decorated
tray. Look out for small gift boxes—perfect for cuff
links or jewelry. Decorate the lid with heart-
shaped tissue-paper confetti, and seal with a twist
of silver wire threaded with leaf-shaped sequins.

ABOVE Scatter the tray with paper rose petals
cut from double crêpe paper—ideal for shaping.
Use the back of a spoon as a mold.

of deep-purple violets enveloped in dark-green ivy. Cards and flowers are still popular today, but, instead of buying them, make your own cards for that intimate touch. Simply wrap garden flowers or the customary red roses in layers of tissue or swathes of the sheerest papers.

LEFT Uplift the traditional red-rose posy using a wrap of simple white tissue paper, scalloped at the edge and decorated with pink and red cutout paper hearts.

OPPOSITE TOP Nothing touches the heart more than a handmade Valentine's card. Decorate a blank greeting card with photocopies of old love letters. Cut a heart shape into the card and add contrast by sticking a slightly larger heart of red tissue paper behind this window.

OPPOSITE MAIN PICTURE
Pamper your lover on Valentine's Day. Bathe with essential oils blended for romance, and relax by candlelight. Glass votive holders are easily dressed up with delicate paper lace. Simply cut a strip the height of the glass holder, curl around, and stick with double-sided tape.

This is the time for the personal touch.
Forget plastic-covered flowers and wrap
yours in tissue scattered with love hearts

from the heart

OPPOSITE A colorful paper hanging provides a lively backdrop for a children's party, and inspires the color theme for the table setting and decorations. A plain paper tablecloth can be transformed by adding a bright runner and cutting a shaped border along the edge. Don't be too precious—cutting free-style makes it quick and easy.

THIS PAGE Children love dressing up for parties. Paper ears attached to headbands and dotted paper scarves are easy to make and enjoyable to wear.

COLORFUL FUN

children's

party

Have fun making simple paper decorations for parties.

Experiment with different papers and make hats, masks,

flags, and toys that are both skillful and amusing.

Explore the excitement of paper with kids.
Storybooks are full of adventures, so pick
a theme to weave your designs around

from alligator to zebra

SEEN ON PAGE 120 Reminiscent
of royal celebrations, paper
bunting is great for special
occasions, and quick to make
from squares of gummed paper.
Simply fold diagonally over
string or twine to make
triangles, and stick along the
bottom edge. Leave a margin
of unstuck paper next to the
string, so the flags can move
freely. Intersperse the flags with
curls of colored streamers.

Parties are always exciting occasions for both children
and adults. With children, time is going to be short, so
disposable plates, paper napkins, and throwaway
tablecloths make good sense and mean that things won't
get broken. Involve the children in designing their party
decorations and dressing the table. Choose bright colors,
lively imagery, and follow a favorite theme—anything from
a fairy tale, football team, or the latest toy, to zoo animals
and cartoon characters. The nature of the decorations
can also help determine the types of papers you use.

ABOVE AND OPPOSITE TOP
LEFT These animal-mad children
loved rubber-stamping—quicker
and easier than stenciling. Mix
nontoxic paint on an artists'
palette or plate, and apply an
even coat to your stamp using
a square of sponge or foam.
Press stamps firmly on colored
art and poster papers. When
dry, cut out and stick to the
edges of paper cups and plates
(not where food will be placed).

RIGHT AND BOTTOM Candy-filled paper cones make original leaving gifts. These are 8 x 10in (20 x 25cm) sheets of colored paper, edged with an alternative border and animal decorations. Twist into a cone, secure with double-sided tape, and punch holes for a raffia handle.

SPOOKY HATS AND NIGHT LIGHTS
Halloween

The magic of Halloween: full moons, bright gold stars, and fiery Chinese lanterns light up chilly fall nights, and the thrill of dressing up fills the air with excitement.

Adults enjoy Halloween just as much as children; making costumes and lanterns is an opportunity for fantasy and make-believe. Masks and costumes were a traditional part of theater, and today can be used for Halloween masquerades and parties. It's the perfect time to dazzle in a witches' hat and cape.

ABOVE AND OPPOSITE Halloween outfits are fun for children to help with. To make a witches' hat, take a black paper cone and cut tabs around its bottom. Glue the tabs to a black poster-board brim and decorate with bright moons and stars. The matching cape, made from

Japanese Mizutamashi paper, has a ribbon threaded around its top to gather into folds. RIGHT Vibrant orange and black Chinese paper lanterns, hung in trees, add an eerie touch to the yard. Suspend paper spiders from the bottom of the lantern to give guests a fright.

FAR RIGHT Candle
bags are great for
lighting the yard at
Halloween. Glue on
black paper bats
and moons to get in
the spirit, and place
the candles in glass
jars for safety.

suppliers

PAPER AND CARD

Most art and stationery stores have a good stock of paper and board, plus paint, glue, and so on.

Alpine Creative Group
28 West 27th Street
4th Floor
New York
NY 10001
(212) 213-8289
Japanese and Indian papers, plus engraving and calligraphy.

Art Essentials
sbart.essentials.com
info@sbartessentials.com
Artists' materials, paper and board, and decorative papers.

Craf-T-Pedlars
1009-D Shary Circle
Concord
CA 94518
(877) PEDLARS
www.pedlars.com
Handmade paper and ribbon.

Crane & Co.
30 South Street
Dalton
MA 01226
(413) 684-2600
www.crane.com
Fine cotton papers, personal stationery, fine art supplies, and tree-free papers.

JAM Paper
For a store near you, call (800) 8010-JAM
www.jampaper.com
Papers of all sizes, envelopes, and customized rubber stamps.

Kate's Paperie
561 Broadway
New York
NY 10012
(212) 941-9816
Over 40,000 papers, many handmade, plus cards, journals, and wrapping.

RIBBONS, TRIMMINGS, AND PAPER TABLEWARE

Paper ribbons are available in every color and width. Fun paper accessories will give a decorative boost to the table.

Bill's Flower Market Inc.
816 Sixth Avenue
New York
NY 10001
(212) 889-8154
Artificial birds, foods, and flowers.

Cape Cod Crafters
Route 1
Freeport
ME 04032
(207) 865-1691
www.capecodcrafters.com
Ribbons, candles, and table decorations, from 11 stores all over New England.

Corz
910B Buccaneer Drive
Glenview
IL 60025
(847) 724-2947
www.corz.com
Table decorations.

Petals
For a store near you, call (800) 920-6000
www.petals.com
Decorative flowers and accessories.

The Ribbonerie
191 Potrero Avenue
San Francisco
CA 94103
(415) 626-6184
www.theribbonerie.com
Specialty ribbon store. All kinds of ribbons from around the world.

Surprise Surprise
91 Third Avenue
New York
NY 10012
(212) 777-0990
Paper plates, napkins, and plastic utensils in all colors.

STATIONERY

A vast choice of stationery is available, and many stores offer a design service.

Blacker & Kooby Stationers
1204 Madison Avenue
New York
NY 10128
(212) 369-8308
Fine papers, calligraphy, and invitations.

Carlson Craft
1750 Tower Boulevard
North Mankato
MN 56003
(800) 774-6848
www.carlsoncraft.com
All kinds of personalized stationery from cards to wedding invitations.

Gabriel Editions
P.O. Box 633
New York
NY 10021
(800) 998-1133
www.gabrieleditions.com
Colorful fun stationery, plus
custom-printing service.

Hudson Street Papers
357 Bleecker Street
New York
NY 10014
Unusual books, stationery,
and housewares.

Il Papiro
1021 Lexington Avenue
New York
NY 10021
(212) 288-9330
Italian stationery and
marbled papers.

Ordning & Reda
253 Colombus Avenue
New York
NY 10023
(212) 799-0828
Handmade paper from
Sweden. Stationery,
notebooks, and giftwrapping.

Sukie
www.sukie.co.uk
Darrell Gibbs' handmade
rescued-paper notebooks.

Willow Tree Lane
For a retailer near you, call
(800) 219-9230
www.willowtreelane.com
Invitations and accessories.

CRAFT SUPPLIERS
AND SPECIALISTS
Good for specialized items
used in this book, such as
transfer medium and Nature
Print paper.

The Art Store
www.artstores.com
Call 1-800-5-GO-ARTS for
store details
Artists' materials, paper, and
easels. Locations nationwide.

**The English Stamp
Company**
Worth Matravers
Dorset BH19 3JP
England
t. (0044) 1929 439117
f. (0044) 1929 439150
sales@englishstamp.com
www.englishstamp.com
Stamp kits with designs from
ferns and scallops to holly
and mistletoe. They also sell
nontoxic paints and custom-
make stamps. Mail order
service available.

Homecrafts Direct
PO Box 38
Leicester LE1 9BU
England
t. (0044) 116 251 3139
f. (0044) 116 251 4452
info@homecrafts.co.uk
www.homecrafts.co.uk
Over 9,000 art and craft items
including photographic Nature
Print paper, paper eggs and
papyrus paper. Mail order and
online shopping available.

**Potpourri Artist's
Supply Inc.**
www.potpourri-art.com
18,000 items of art and craft
materials to buy online.

PAPER FOR INTERIORS
Designers have introduced
paper into the home for
screens, rugs, wallpaper,
and lighting.

Interiors bis
60 Sloane Avenue
London SW3 3DD
England
t. (0044) 20 7838 1104
An inspirational shop for
lovers of interiors. Check
out their Interior Carton
cardboard screens.

Mint
70 Wigmore Street
London W1U 2SF
England
t. (0044) 20 7224 4406
Unusual designer home
goods. Mint stock paper-
flower fairy lights, Pierre
Pozzi paper trays, baskets,
lighting, and more.

SKK
34 Lexington Street
London W1F 0LH
England
t. (0044) 20 7434 4095
Shiu-Kay Kan's architectural
lighting consultancy. A
stockist of cutting-edge
lighting design.

ARTISTS AND DESIGNERS
There is a wealth of artists
and designers who work in
paper. I have included some
of this inspirational work.

Lorraine Dawkins
t. (0044) 20 7378 7868
Lorraine's wonderful cards
are handmade using silk-
screened images printed
on thick tracing paper or
collaged Chinese papers
secured with raffia.

Lynn Dennison
Flowers East Gallery
119–205 Richmond Road
London E8 3NJ
England
t. (0044) 20 8985 3333
Inspired by fairy stories,
Lynn's amazing sculptural
shoes and dresses appeal to
the child in all of us.

Magie Hollingworth
t. (0044) 1623 481102
Magie loves recycling paper,
and uses papier-mâché as a
perfect vehicle for expression,
making stunning bowls and
wall decorations.

Andrea Joynson
t. (0044) 20 8697 1524
Andrea takes her inspiration
from gardening and period
costumes, bringing bags
up to date using paper as a
base fabric.

Libby Lister
t. (0044) 1460 64605
Libby has rejuvenated the
ancient craft of paper-flower
making, using crêpe papers
hand-tinted with watercolors.

Judy Simmons
t. (0044) 20 8464 5378
Brightly colored and modern,
Judy's bowls and papier-
mâché animals are treasures.

USEFUL BOOKS
The Book of Fine Paper
by Silvie Turner
Thames and Hudson (1998)

The Paper Shoe Book
by Julian Horsey and Chris
Knowles
Ebury Press (1995, currently
out of print)
Paper patterns and directions
for making paper shoes.

Acknowledgments

The author and publisher would like to thank the following people for allowing us to photograph
in their homes: Marian Cotterill, Frazer Cunningham, Gillian Rowe, and Ros Fairman.

My first big thankyou will have to go to Polly Wreford for taking such
inspirational pictures, and for helping to maintain a wonderful sense
of calm throughout the photography days. Thank you also to her
assistant Matt for being very hands-on in the "making department."

A special thankyou goes to Louisa Grey, my assistant, for all her
tireless support and energy, and Nel Haynes and Lorraine Dawkins
for enthusiastically giving up several days to help decorate Easter
eggs and bonnets!

A huge thankyou to my family and friends for their constant
support and encouragement, despite me talking of little else for
at least six months!

I am eternally grateful to the many people who kindly lent their work
and props for the shoot, and to the patience of my wonderful child
models: Dylan, Felix, Alexandra, Yasemin, and Scarlett.

Finally I would like to thank everyone at Ryland Peters & Small, who
have worked so hard to produce *Paper Details*: Alison Starling,
Gabriella Le Grazie, Clare Double, Sally Powell, Kate Brunt, and
Sarah Hepworth.